MY GUIDE TO US CITIZENSHIP

US IMMIGRATION SERVICES

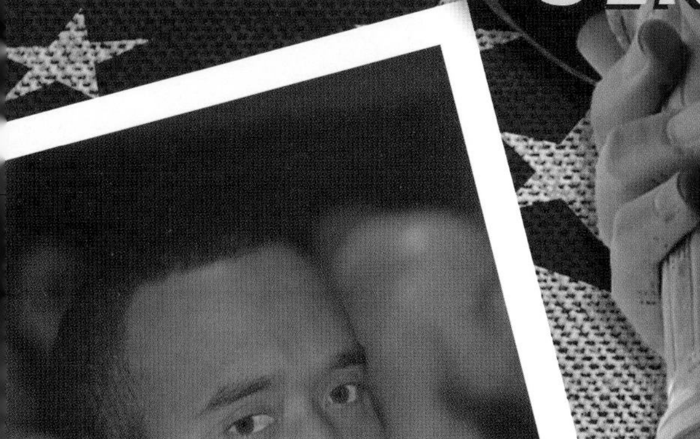

Amie Jane Leavitt

Mitchell Lane
PUBLISHERS
P.O. Box 196
Hockessin, DE 19707
www.mitchellane.com

Mitchell Lane
PUBLISHERS

MY GUIDE TO
US CITIZENSHIP

Immigration in the US
US Immigration Services
US Laws of Citizenship
Your Guide to Becoming a US Citizen

PUBLISHER'S NOTE: The facts on which this book is based have been thoroughly researched. Documentation of such research can be found on page 44. While every possible effort has been made to ensure accuracy, the publisher will not assume liability for damages caused by inaccuracies in the data, and makes no warranty on the accuracy of the information contained herein.

The Internet sites referenced herein were active as of the publication date. Due to the fleeting nature of some web sites, we cannot guarantee that they will all be active when you are reading this book.

NOTE FROM THE AUTHOR: A special thanks to Wesley Biutanaseva, Fraser Smith, and Silvano Sbarra who agreed to be interviewed for this book. Your contributions were immensely appreciated and your experiences through the immigration process helped provide a personal flavor to the text.

Printing   1   2   3   4   5   6   7   8   9

Library of Congress
Leavitt, Amie Jane.
 US immigration services / by Amie Jane Leavitt.
    pages cm. — (My guide to US citizenship)
 Includes bibliographical references and index.
 ISBN 978-1-61228-447-7 (library bound)
1. Emigration and immigration—United States—Juvenile literature. 2. Emigration and immigration law—United States—Juvenile literature. I. Title. II. Title: United States immigration services.
 JV6483.L42 2013
 325.73—dc23
                                    2013023008
eBook ISBN: 9781612285078

PLB

CONTENTS

Words in **bold** appear in the Glossary.

The United States is a land of immigrants. Just about every country of the world is represented in our citizenry.

A Country of Immigrants

An immigrant is a person who comes to live permanently in a foreign country. Immigrants are part of the population of just about every country in the world, especially the United States. In fact, the United States is a country that is made up almost entirely of immigrants. Everyone living in the United States today—with the exception of Native Americans—is either an immigrant or the **descendant** of an immigrant. It could be argued by some that even the Native Americans should be considered immigrants, too. That's because at some point long ago in their history, they came to this land from somewhere else.

In today's world, people immigrate to the United States for a variety of reasons. Some come to get an education, like Wesley

Biutanaseva did when he came here from Fiji. He had been attending a technical school there to become a plumber. His dad was using his retirement money to pay for Biutanaseva's tuition at this very expensive school. But even after paying hefty tuition fees and working hard to complete his education, Biutanaseva would still only have a certificate and not a degree. Even this certificate was not a guarantee that he would be able to find a job in Fiji.

Biutanaseva looked around at some other options. He applied to Brigham Young University—Hawaii, a school that specializes in educating **international** students. About 2,500 students attend school there, coming from more than seventy countries. Although Biutanaseva was accepted as a student

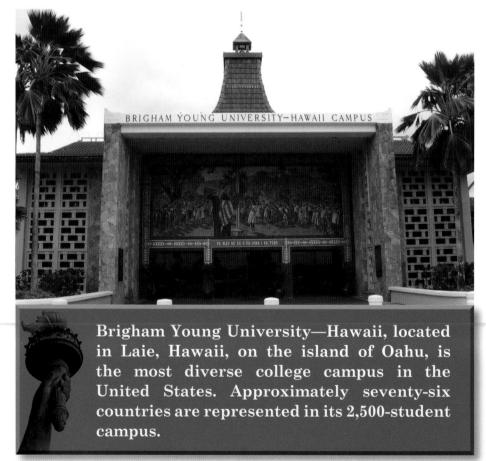

Brigham Young University—Hawaii, located in Laie, Hawaii, on the island of Oahu, is the most diverse college campus in the United States. Approximately seventy-six countries are represented in its 2,500-student campus.

at BYU—Hawaii, he still needed permission from the United States government to enter the country. This permission is called a **visa**. As a student, he had to show the United States government that he had a way to pay for his housing and food. Biutanaseva was able to achieve this with the help of The Polynesian Culture Center (PCC). This tourist attraction features shows and exhibits and is owned by the same church that owns BYU-Hawaii. The PCC regularly offers jobs to BYU-Hawaii students so that they can pay for their living expenses.[1]

Other people come to the United States for family reasons. Silvano Sbarra is an immigrant from Milan, Italy. He lived there with his wife and child, and had a great job. But his wife, a California native, missed American life. They decided to move to the United States, but Sbarra had to first get approval from the US government. Since Sbarra was married to a United States citizen, this approval was much easier to get than it is for most people. Still, it took a long time. He had to fill out a lot of paperwork and wait, and wait, and wait. Three years passed before the government granted him permission to move to the United States and work here.[2]

Other immigrants come to the United States for other reasons. Some come for work that they can't find in their own country. Some come because their family members are

Every ten years in the United States, a census is taken to find out information about the country's population. In 2010, the census showed that the immigrant population in the United States was nearly forty million, or 13 percent of the total population. The percentage of immigrants in the United States hasn't been that high since the early 1900s.[3]

According to the 2010 census, nearly seventeen million children in this country have at least one parent who is an immigrant.[4]

already here and they want to join them. Some come because their homelands are dangerous places and they need to escape. Some come for freedom from terrible governments. Some come because they were adopted by US citizens or marry US citizens. Some come because they've heard that the United States is a "land of milk and honey" and they want to see their dreams come true. These reasons are not new to immigrants today—for hundreds of years, these factors have motivated people from all over the world to move to the United States.

Not everyone who wants to come to the United States today gets to do so, though. And, in fact, there have been restrictions on immigration from just about the very beginning. Even the Mayflower Pilgrims had to either have the money to pay for their passage on the ship or they had to promise to work to pay their debt as **indentured servants**. Just as money was a restriction for them and other early immigrants, money is still a restriction for immigrants today. The government imposes other restrictions, as well.

The government places restrictions on immigration for many reasons. One of those reasons is that the United States has limited resources. There are only a certain number of jobs available in the United States. Many immigrants from poorer countries are willing to do the same job as an American for less pay—many people believe that this leaves American citizens without jobs. There are also only so many places available for people to live. And there is also only a specific amount of government funding—which comes from taxes—available to pay for education, healthcare, and other services. Many people feel that if an unlimited number of

Many of the first immigrants to the United States came here for religious freedom, like the pilgrims on the Mayflower as shown in this lithograph by Currier and Ives.

people were allowed to move to the United States each year, there wouldn't be enough resources to support them and the people who already live here. On the other hand, immigrants pay for their food, housing, and other basic needs. The money that they spend at local businesses helps to create more jobs in their communities. Immigrants pay taxes, as well, allowing the government to provide more services to all citizens.

The government also has to restrict immigration for safety reasons. There are some people who want to come to the United States to commit crimes. On September 11, 2001, terrorists were able to enter our country and kill thousands of people. The government has to make sure that the people who come here have good intentions and want to better the country—not hurt it or its citizens.

Silvano Sbarra and his family celebrated on the day he became a United States citizen.

Coming to the USA

So, let's say a person living in another country wants to immigrate to the United States. What does this person need to do? What steps are necessary for the person to take?

The process is different for every person. It all depends on the reasons they are coming here and what they hope to accomplish.

Before Italian immigrant Silvano Sbarra came to the United States in 2009, he applied for his **green card**.[1] This card is just an official document that says that an immigrant has the legal right to live and work in the United States. It is proof of permanent residence. It usually lasts for ten years, and then the resident has to reapply. A green card also lets a person apply for US citizenship later on.

Most people obtain their green cards in one of three ways. People who have an **immediate family** member who is already a US citizen or permanent resident can apply for a green card with their **sponsorship**. Others may have a job offer in the United States. Those people can also apply, with sponsorship from the employer. Still others are entitled to apply if they are refugees who cannot go back to their own country because of war or unsafe conditions.

Sbarra was married to a US citizen, so he could apply for his green card with her sponsorship. In order to find out how to apply, he did a search on the internet. He found official US government agency websites. He read the information

UNITED STATES OF AMERICA PERMANENT RESIDENT

SPECIMEN TEST V 01 JAN 1920

Surname
SPECIMEN

Given Name
TEST V

USCIS#
000-000-001

Category
RE8

Country of Birth
Utopia

Date of Birth
01 JAN 1920

Sex
F

Card Expires: **08/21/07**
Resident Since: **08/21/07**

Test V. Specimen

A "green card" allows a citizen of another country to live and work legally in the United States.

on these websites and downloaded the forms he needed to fill out. He visited the American consulate to be fingerprinted which allowed the US government to check his background and make sure he hadn't broken any laws. Once Sbarra had completed all of his paperwork and fingerprinting, he mailed his application to a US Customs and Immigration Services office.[2]

Some Other Ways to Get a Green Card

These are a few of the other categories of people who might be eligible for a green card:

- Amerasian child of a US citizen (generally a child of an Armed Forces member)
- American Indian born in Canada
- Armed Forces member
- Cuban native or citizen
- Person born to a foreign diplomat in the United States
- Person from a country with a low rate of immigration to the United States (Diversity Immigrant Visa Program)
- Victim of criminal activity
- Witness or informant to an American law enforcement agency[3]

After Sbarra sent in his paperwork, he had to wait. Months went by. Then he received his packet back in the mail. He opened the envelope and read a letter that explained that he needed to change his application. Sbarra had followed all the directions when he sent in the application. But things had changed since he sent it in, so his application wasn't up to date anymore.

Sbarra filled out the paperwork again and sent it back. Then, he waited again. Months went by again. Then, he received his packet back in the mail a second time. It was the same story. Once again, something had changed in the process and so his application wasn't complete anymore.

This cycle happened over and over again. Each time, he had to fill out a new version of a form, sign a new document, or pay more money. In the end, that is why it took three years for his application to be processed.[4] For some people, though, it can take much longer. Being married to a US citizen actually helps things move faster!

This experience isn't unique to Sbarra. Many immigrants actually get their paperwork bounced back and forth several times.

Fraser Smith, a Canadian who immigrated to the United States in 1985, said his experience with paperwork more than twenty years ago was the most frustrating part of his immigration process. "I got my green card application sent back to me three times. When they sent it back, it could be because something had changed in [the government's] process. You'd get the whole thing back and then maybe you'd have to fill out one form and then send the whole thing back again," Smith explained.[5]

Once Sbarra finished all his paperwork, he was invited to the US consulate in Naples, Italy. While there, he was given a complete medical examination. He received a lot of shots for immunizations, even though he had proof that he had already received those shots as a child. He had to sign a paper that said that if anything happened to him because of the shots, the US government was not responsible for it. He even received a psychological examination to make sure he did not have a mental illness.

Once he passed this medical examination, he was scheduled for an interview for the next day. He had to bring all of his paperwork. The officials at the consulate looked over his paperwork very carefully. They asked him questions to make sure that his marriage to his US-citizen wife was real and legal.

After everything went okay in the interview, he was sent to another area where he had to pay more fees. It cost about $1,500 to process all of his paperwork. He paid his money and then he sat in line and waited again. Finally, he was called up to the desk. "They gave me a stamp in my Italian passport. It said I had six months to get to the United States and my green card would be issued to me there," Sbarra explained.[6]

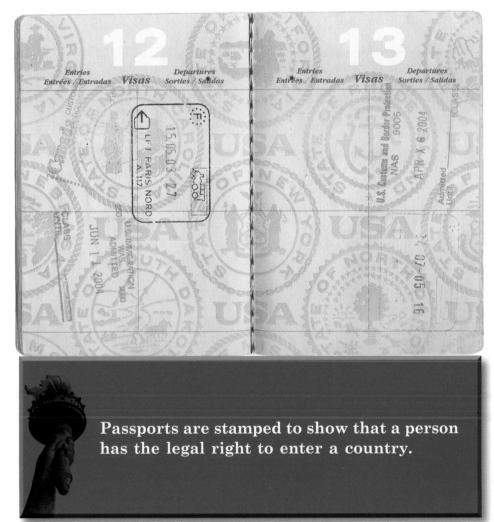

Passports are stamped to show that a person has the legal right to enter a country.

Responsibilities of Permanent Residents

A person who has a green card is required to do certain things. Having a green card is a privilege, not a right. That privilege can be taken away if a person doesn't follow the rules and obey the law. These responsibilities are:

- Must not leave the United States for an extended period of time or move to another country to live there permanently.
- Obey the law.
- File federal, state, and local income tax returns.
- Males between the ages of eighteen and twenty-six must register with the Selective Service (military draft).
- Maintain their immigration status.
- Carry their green card at all times.
- Permanent residents who move must give their new address to the Department of Homeland Security (DHS).[7]

Rights of Permanent Residents

Green card holders have certain rights available to them. They can:

- Live and work permanently anywhere in the United States.
- Apply to become a US citizen once they are eligible.
- Request visas for a husband or wife and unmarried children to live in the United States.
- Get a Social Security number.
- Receive Social Security, Supplemental Security Income, and Medicare benefits, if they are eligible.
- Own property in the United States
- Apply for a driver's license in their state or territory.
- Leave and return to the United States under certain conditions.
- Attend public school and college.
- Join certain branches of the US Armed Forces.
- Purchase or own a firearm, as long as there are no state or local restrictions which prohibit it.[8]

The President of the United States has the job of selecting cabinet members. President Barack Obama selected John Kerry as secretary of state. Kerry was sworn in on February 1, 2013.

Services Available to Immigrants

There are many services available to people who want to immigrate to the United States. According to many people who have been through the immigration process themselves, the best place to go is the Internet.

The United States government has several official websites that provide immigrants with the information they need. One of these is operated by the US Department of State and another is operated by the US Department of Homeland Security.

The president of the United States is responsible for appointing cabinet members to head different federal departments. Two of these cabinet members are the secretary of state and the secretary of homeland security. These officials and their

In the United States, the Department of Homeland Security is responsible for immigration and border security. Here, Secretary of Homeland Security Janet Napolitano talks about these issues on February 5, 2013.

office staff work together in the immigration process. Their job in immigration is to provide the proper resources for people who want to come here legally. They are also responsible for ensuring that the people who come here do so with good intentions. These departments take their responsibilities very seriously.

The US State Department's immigration-related website is travel.state.gov. This website has information for people who just want to be temporary visitors to the United States—tourists. This site also has detailed information for people who want to come to the United States on a permanent basis—immigrants. The site provides information about how to find United States embassies in countries around the world. It answers questions about visas and explains how to apply for visas. It also gives reasons why someone might be denied a visa. It publishes statistics on the number of visas that are given out every year.

Another great website is US Citizenship and Immigration Services found at http://www.uscis.gov. This website, run by the US Department of Homeland Security, has information on becoming a permanent resident and working in the country. It also has instructions on how an immigrant can become a citizen. There is information explaining how a person who is a refugee in his or her country can immigrate to the United States for safety. The site also explains how a United States citizen can legally adopt children from other countries. People can find all of the forms they need for immigration

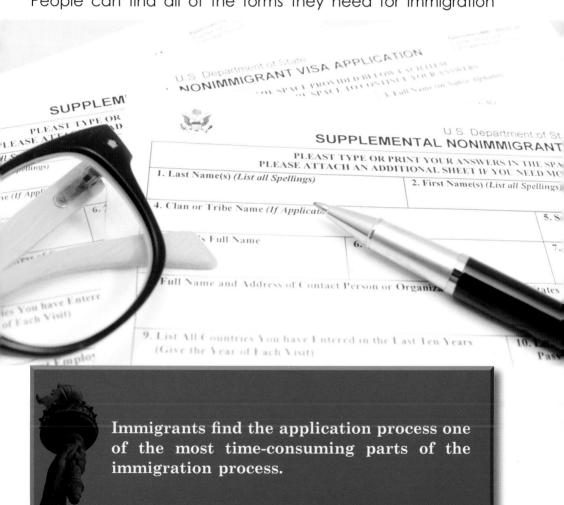

Immigrants find the application process one of the most time-consuming parts of the immigration process.

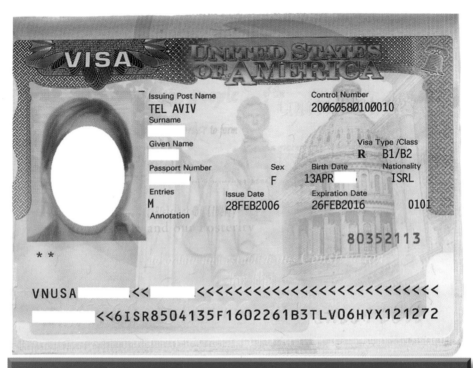

Issuing Post Name		**Control Number**
TEL AVIV		200605801000010
Surname		
Given Name		**Visa Type /Class**
		R B1/B2
Passport Number	**Sex**	**Birth Date** **Nationality**
	F	13APR ISRL
Entries	**Issue Date**	**Expiration Date**
M	28FEB2006	26FEB2016 0101
Annotation		

80352113

* *

VNUSA   <<   <<<<<<<<<<<<<<<<<<<<<<<<<<
             <<6ISR8504135F1602261B3TLV06HYX121272

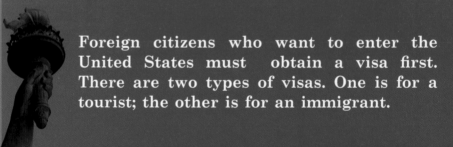

Foreign citizens who want to enter the United States must obtain a visa first. There are two types of visas. One is for a tourist; the other is for an immigrant.

and citizenship on this website. These forms can be downloaded, filled out on a computer, printed, signed, and then mailed in to the appropriate address.

Not everything can be done online, though. Some things (like fingerprints, medical examinations, and interviews) must be done in person at a US embassy, consulate, or diplomatic mission. Some cities have embassies. Some have consulates, and some have diplomatic missions. Embassies are usually located in the capital cities of foreign countries. Generally, immigrants can complete their visa requirements at any of these official United States government locations.

Once people have immigrated to the United States and have become permanent residents, there are other places that they can go to get the additional help they need. There are community and church groups that offer assistance to immigrants. There are state and local agencies. There are also federal agencies that can help, too, like US Citizenship and Immigration Services, the Department of State, and the Department of Education.[1]

There are local USCIS (United States Citizenship and Immigration Services) offices in nearly every one of the fifty states plus the US territories (Guam, Puerto Rico, and the Virgin Islands).

U.S. Citizenship and Immigration Services

Federal Agencies with Immigration and Integration Responsibilities

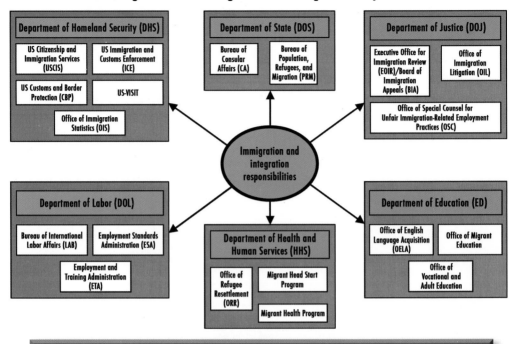

Department of Homeland Security (DHS)
- US Citizenship and Immigration Services (USCIS)
- US Immigration and Customs Enforcement (ICE)
- US Customs and Border Protection (CBP)
- US-VISIT
- Office of Immigration Statistics (OIS)

Department of State (DOS)
- Bureau of Consular Affairs (CA)
- Bureau of Population, Refugees, and Migration (PRM)

Department of Justice (DOJ)
- Executive Office for Immigration Review (EOIR)/Board of Immigration Appeals (BIA)
- Office of Immigration Litigation (OIL)
- Office of Special Counsel for Unfair Immigration-Related Employment Practices (OSC)

Immigration and integration responsibilities

Department of Labor (DOL)
- Bureau of International Labor Affairs (LAB)
- Employment Standards Administration (ESA)
- Employment and Training Administration (ETA)

Department of Health and Human Services (HHS)
- Office of Refugee Resettlement (ORR)
- Migrant Head Start Program
- Migrant Health Program

Department of Education (ED)
- Office of English Language Acquisition (OELA)
- Office of Migrant Education
- Office of Vocational and Adult Education

> Federal agencies each have different responsibilities in relation to immigration and citizenship.

New permanent residents generally need help finding housing, locating child care and education for their kids, learning English, opening a bank account, finding a job, obtaining health care, and getting a driver's license. They also may need help in times of emergency (fire, police, or ambulance) and will need to know what to do at those times.

The US Citizenship and Immigration Services department publishes a guidebook for new permanent residents called "Welcome to the United States: A Guide for New Immigrants." This 124-page guidebook goes through many of the things

Welcome to the United States
A Guide for New Immigrants

U.S. Citizenship
and Immigration
Services

M-618 (rev. 09/07)

that new immigrants might need help with and where they can go to receive that help. This guidebook is available to download online.[2]

Another resource for new immigrants is the Welcome to USA website at http://www.welcometousa.gov. This site helps people find places to learn English in their area. It also gives suggestions for immigrants who need help finding daycare, schools, housing, banks, and jobs. The site even gives immigrants the links to information on becoming a United States citizen.

New immigrants, and people wanting to become immigrants, need to be very careful of fraud. There are companies and individuals that try to take advantage of immigrants. When visiting websites related to immigration, it's always best to stick with ones that end in ".gov." This ending means that they are official United States government websites. If additional help is required, there are certified immigration attorneys who are available for hire as well.

In the 2010 census, nearly 40 million people said they were immigrants. Of that number, 53 percent said they were from Latin America or the Caribbean—about 21.2 million people.[3]

Naturalization ceremonies can be an emotional time for those who have made it through the long immigration and citizenship process.

Pathway to Citizenship

Once a person has a green card for a specific number of years, he or she can start working towards **naturalization**. This means that he or she can become a US citizen.

If you are filing on your own without the sponsorship of another citizen, you have to wait five years. If you have a spouse who is an American citizen, you only have to wait three years. If you are a military member or the spouse or child of a military member, you can become a citizen even faster (depending upon your individual situation).[1]

Wesley Biutanaseva could have applied for United States citizenship after three years since his wife was a US citizen. However, he decided that he wanted to file on his own, so he waited until the five-year mark.[2]

Biutanaseva explained that this part of the process was much easier than applying for the green card. "I had to fill out a ton of paperwork for my permanent residency. I had to include tax forms, background checks, and many other things," he explained, showing a huge folder of paperwork that was at least three inches thick. "I didn't have to fill out this paperwork again. The process was much easier to become a citizen than a permanent resident—at least it was for me."[3]

He did have to have his fingerprints taken and checked again. "The government has to make sure you haven't broken any laws during the five years that you've been a permanent resident," he explained. "If I had done anything wrong or had broken the law during that time, I might have been denied citizenship."[4]

Once you pass the fingerprinting, you will want to start studying for the tests you will have to take in a few months. You will have to take an English speaking test, an English reading test, an English writing test, and a civics test.

Naturalization Citizenship Test
The civics test can include any of one hundred possible questions. There are questions about American government, American history, and American geography. Here are some examples:

- What is the supreme law of the land?
- What did the Declaration of Independence do?
- Who is one of your state's US senators now?
- Why did the colonists fight the British?
- What is the name of the national anthem?[5]

The immigration department gave Biutanaseva a CD with all of the questions and answers for the civics test on it. "I listened to it in my car every day for two months as I drove back and forth to work," Biutanaseva explained. "I wanted to make sure I knew all of the answers perfectly. My friends who had taken it had said how easy it was. I didn't want to fail it and look bad."[6]

On the day of the interview, the prospective citizen should be dressed in proper attire. A naturalization officer conducts the interview, and begins by placing the person under an oath to tell the truth. The officer will review the application, asking questions to make sure that everything is correct. For the English test, the interviewer first asks the person to read a sentence in English. Then, the person has to write a sentence or two in English. The civics test will follow, with ten questions from a list of one hundred possible questions. The person must answer six correctly. If he or she misses more than four questions, another interview is scheduled. "If after the second interview, you still can't pass the civics test, then they'll send you a letter that pretty much says 'Sorry buddy,'" Biutanaseva explained.[7]

Yet, Biutanaseva didn't have to worry about receiving a letter like this. Neither did Silvano Sbarra or Fraser Smith. They all passed the interview and tests on their first try.[8]

After the interview is finished, the officer may give a date for the naturalization ceremony. Other times, the date and location for this event may come in the mail. This ceremony is where immigrants officially become citizens of the United States. People need to dress appropriately for the ceremony, just like they did for the interview.

"Out of the thirty-one people who were becoming citizens on the day I was," Sbarra explains, "there were twenty-seven different countries. People were here from China, South Africa, Chile, France, Spain, Germany. It was an emotional time. Many people cried." The reason it was so emotional, he believes, is because people really appreciate their new citizenship. It takes a lot of work and time to immigrate to the United States and to become a citizen. People cry

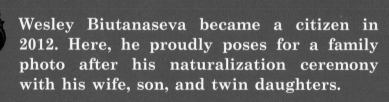
Wesley Biutanaseva became a citizen in 2012. Here, he proudly poses for a family photo after his naturalization ceremony with his wife, son, and twin daughters.

because they are so happy that their dream finally came true for them.[9]

At the ceremony, there may be speeches by senators and other important people. The new citizens say the Pledge of Allegiance to the United States flag and a judge then asks the new citizens to stand up and read the Oath of Allegiance. Once the oath has been sworn, all of the new citizens get a certificate that shows they are now citizens of the United States.

Oath of Allegiance

This is the Oath of Allegiance that new US citizens must take:

"I hereby declare, on oath, that I absolutely and entirely renounce and abjure all allegiance and fidelity to any foreign prince, potentate, state or sovereignty, of whom or which I have heretofore been a subject or citizen; that I will support and defend the Constitution and laws of the United States of America against all enemies, foreign and domestic; that I will bear true faith and allegiance to the same; that I will bear arms on behalf of the United States when required by the law; that I will perform noncombatant service in the armed forces of the United States when required by the law; that I will perform work of national importance under civilian direction when required by the law; and that I take this obligation freely without any mental reservation or purpose of evasion; so help me God."[10]

People who want to become US citizens must meet the following criteria:

- are at least eighteen years old
- have lived continuously in the US as a permanent resident
- have shown "good moral character"
- have passed the English and civics exams
- have paid an application fee[11]

In the twenty-first century, immigration is a big issue in many states, especially those bordering Mexico. Here, Mexican immigrants marched to protect their rights in 2006 in San Jose, California.

Controlling Immigration

According to the American Immigration Council, the United States immigration system has historically "been based upon three principles: the reunification of families, admitting immigrants with skills that are valuable to the US economy, and protecting refugees."[1]

The family unification piece of the system allows US citizens to **sponsor** their immediate family members: spouses, unmarried minor children under age twenty-one, and parents. There are no limits to the number of these visas that can be given out every year. There, are however, limits to the number of visas given out to brothers and sisters and adult children of US citizens. There are also limits to the number of visas offered to the spouses and minor children of permanent residents. Obviously, then, the easiest way for a person to immigrate to the United States is to marry a US citizen. But don't think that idea is a new one. People have been trying this for years, and the immigration department watches such things very closely to make sure that all marriages are legitimate and real.

Since the family unification part of the immigration system is nearly unlimited, the rest of the immigration system must have restrictions. A limited number of immigrant visas are given out every year for workers and refugees.

Workers who have advanced degrees and special skills have a better chance of being able to immigrate. Fraser Smith fell into that category. He had a PhD (which he attained from a school in the United States). Because of this, he fell into the top tier of workers who are allowed into the United States. He had to prove, though, that there wasn't a US citizen who was capable of doing his job. "I had to place a job ad for the position I was qualified for in a nationally-read journal and deal with all of the responses, if any."[2]

Every year, the president of the United States and Congress announce the number of people who can come into the country as refugees. In 2013, the limit was seventy thousand. That number was divided among the regions of the world (Africa, East Asia, Europe and Central Asia, Latin America and the Caribbean, and the Near East and South Asia).[3]

There are also restrictions placed on the number of immigrants allowed per country. According to the US immigration policy, out of all the green cards given out every year, only 7 percent can be given to immigrants from a single country. That number includes family and employment immigrant visas. Let's say, for example, that there are a large number of people living in the United States who are US citizens or permanent residents originally from Mexico. One would expect that each year, a large number of these people would apply for the family-based visas for their

PARA PROBLEMAS LEGALES UNES 8:00 a.m. A 1:00 p.m.

When immigrants arrive with little education, or when they arrive illegally, their options for work are limited. Many accept short-term labor jobs, like the ones that are assigned at the El Centro Humanitario labor office in Denver, Colorado. Here, program director Harrold Lasso conducts a lottery to assign workers to jobs.

immediate family members. Because of this, there are a very limited number of visas left for people who don't have any family connections in the United States. This rule is the same for all countries, but some countries are definitely more impacted by this rule than others. This makes it extremely difficult for a person to immigrate here from certain countries if they don't have immediate family here already.

Another way people can get their immigrant visa is through the Diversity Lottery. This system allows people from certain countries to enter their name into a drawing. Fifty thousand names are drawn by a computer. Those chosen can then apply for permanent residence. There are limits to

In Dhaka, Bangladesh, residents who hope to immigrate to the United States wait in line to mail their entries for the 1996 Diversity Lottery.

this, though. If more than fifty thousand people from your country came to the United States in the last five years, you are not eligible for this lottery. Also, you must have a certain level of education or training to enter.

According to a 2010 article in *USA Today*, a Mexican-born adult son or daughter of a US citizen will likely have to wait eighteen years to come here. Likewise, a person who was born in the Philippines and has a sibling who is a US citizen will have to wait nineteen years to immigrate here.

In the same article it was asked: "So how does an unskilled worker from Mexico, with no job offer and no family in the [United States] get to legally immigrate there?" The answer from an immigration lawyer in Arizona was, "He can't." There just isn't any system set up for people in that situation to come here legally.[4]

Unfortunately, that's likely why so many people choose to cross the border and come to the United States illegally. They know their chances of coming here legally are basically nonexistent.

A sign at the international boundary between Canada and the United States in Point Roberts, Washington

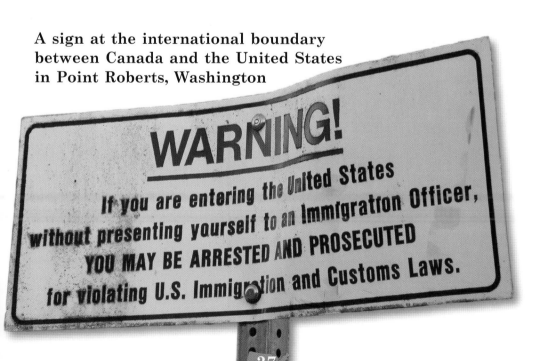

The US-Mexico border is where most illegal immigrants enter the United States.

The border between Nogales, Arizona, and Nogales, Mexico, is considered one of the most dangerous areas along the US-Mexico border.

The Rio Grande River separates Texas from Mexico. This is another common entry point of illegal immigrants.

It's estimated that in 2009, there were a total of 11.1 million illegal immigrants living in this country.[5]

Illegal immigration causes a great deal of problems for the country on many levels. One problem is safety. Since there is no paperwork on illegal immigrants, there's no way to know what their background is. Are they peaceful people who just want a better life for themselves and their families? Maybe. But then again, maybe not. There's just no way to know for sure since they didn't go through the proper process. Entering illegally could be an attractive option to people intending to do harm, since they will avoid having their backgrounds checked this way.

Another way that illegal immigration causes problems for the country is in the distribution of resources. This includes such things as health care, emergency services, and education. For example, according to the California Hospital Association, illegal immigrants cost the hospitals in that state more than $1.25 billion a year.[6] That's because federal law requires that hospitals provide emergency care for every patient who walks through its doors, regardless of their ability to pay.

According to the Department of Homeland Security,

the majority of illegal immigrants in this country come from Mexico.[7] Because of that, fences and border-patrol agents stretch along much of the nearly two-thousand-mile border between the United States and Mexico. Yet, people still try to cross. In San Diego, California, there are signs along the freeway warning drivers that people might be running across. In other places along the border, people tunnel underneath the fences to cross unseen by border patrol agents. They also hide in trucks and other vehicles and try to sneak across the border that way.

Illegal immigration is definitely a serious issue in our country. Something must be done, but lawmakers are not sure what. Some say that the immigration law needs to be updated to allow more people to come here legally. On the other hand, some say that the border needs to be more tightly enforced so fewer immigrants are allowed to come in. Many believe that people caught here illegally need to be **deported**. Others say that people here illegally should not be given services like health care, education, and jobs and then maybe they'd go back home.

Regardless what is done about the current immigration situation in our country, one thing is for sure: the United States will always welcome immigrants to its shores, in one way or another. As it says on a plaque inside the Statue of Liberty, "Give me your tired, your poor, your huddled masses yearning to breathe free!"

Every year, approximately **47 percent** of all illegal border crossings into the United States occur along the **Arizona-Mexico** border.[8]

Chapter 1: A Country of Immigrants
1. Wesley Biutanaseva, personal interview with author, December 2012.
2. Silvano Sbarra, personal interview with author, December 2012.
3. Jeanne Batalova and Alicia Lee, *Migration Information Source*, "US in Focus: Frequently Requested Statistics on Immigrants and Immigration in the United States," March 2012.
4. Ibid.

Chapter 2: Coming to the USA
1. Sbarra, interview.
2. Ibid.
3. US Citizenship and Immigration Services, "Other Ways to Get a Green Card," April 16, 2013.
4. Sbarra, interview.
5. Fraser Smith, personal interview with author, December 2012.
6. Sbarra, interview.
7. US Citizenship and Immigration Services, "Welcome to the United States: A Guide for New Immigrants," September 2007, p. 10.
8. Ibid., p. 8.

Chapter 3: Services Available to Immigrants
1. Megan Davy, et al., *Migration Information Source*, "US in Focus: Who Does What in US Immigration," December 2005.
2. US Citizenship and Immigration Services, "Welcome to the United States: A Guide for New Immigrants," September 2007.
3. Elizabeth M. Grieco, et al., *American Community Survey Reports*, "The Foreign-Born Population in the United States: 2010," May 2012.

Chapter 4: Pathway to Citizenship

1. US Citizenship and Immigration Services, "Citizenship through Naturalization," January 22, 2013.
2. Biutanaseva, interview.
3. Ibid.
4. Ibid.
5. US Citizenship and Immigration Services, "Civics (History and Government) Questions for the Naturalization Test," March 2011.
6. Biutanaseva, interview.
7. Ibid.
8. Biutanaseva, interview; Sbarra, interview; Smith, interview.
9. Sbarra, interview.
10. US Citizenship and Immigration Services, "Naturalization Oath of Allegiance to the United States of America," September 4, 2012.
11. Immigration Policy Center, American Immigration Council, "How the United States Immigration System Works: A Fact Sheet," November 4, 2010.

Chapter 5: Controlling Immigration

1. Immigration Policy Center, American Immigration Council, "How the United States Immigration System Works: A Fact Sheet," November 4, 2010.
2. Smith, interview.
3. Barack Obama, The White House, "Presidential Memorandum—Annual Refugee Admissions Numbers," September 28, 2012.
4. Chris Hawley, USA Today, "Immigration Has Grown More Complicated," October 8, 2010.
5. Ibid.
6. Dave Gibson, Examiner.com, "Illegal Aliens Cost California More Than $1 Billion Annually," July 11, 2011.
7. US Department of Homeland Security, Office of Immigration Statistics, "2011 Yearbook of Immigration Statistics," September 2012.
8. Federation for American Immigration Reform, Immigration Issues, "Immigration in Arizona: Fact Sheet (2012)," April 2012.

Books

Blohm, Judith M., and Terri Lapinsky. *Kids Like Me: Voices of the Immigrant Experience.* Boston: Intercultural Press, 2006.

Bogomolny, Abby. *New to North America: Writing by U.S. Immigrants, Their Children and Grandchildren.* Santa Rosa, CA: Burning Bush Publications, 2007.

Ellis, Deborah. *Children of War: Voices of Iraqi Refugees.* Toronto, Ontario: Groundwood Brooks, 2009.

Miller, Debra A. *Immigration.* Farmington Hills, MI: Greenhaven Press, 2010.

Robinson, Anthony, and Annemarie Young. *Gervelie's Journey: A Refugee Diary.* London: Frances Lincoln Children's Books, 2010.

Roza, Greg. *Immigration and Migration.* New York: Gareth Stevens Publishing, 2011.

On the Internet

My Immigration Story: "The Stories of US Immigrants in Their Own Words"
   http://www.myimmigrationstory.com/
PBS, Independent Lens: "The New Americans"
   http://www.pbs.org/independentlens/newamericans/
US Citizenship and Immigration Services
   http://www.uscis.gov/
US Department of State
   http://travel.state.gov/
Welcome to USA
   http://www.welcometousa.gov/

Works Consulted

Batalova, Jeanne, and Alicia Lee. "US in Focus: Frequently Requested Statistics on Immigrants and Immigration in the United States." *Migration Information Source*, March 2012. http://www.migrationinformation.org/usfocus/display.cfm?ID=886#1

Beaver, Janice Cheryl. "US International Borders: Brief Facts." Congressional Research Service, November 9, 2006. http://www.au.af.mil/au/awc/awcgate/crs/rs21729.pdf

Biutanaseva, Wesley. Personal interview with author, December 2012.

Davy, Megan, Deborah W. Meyers, and Jeanne Batalova. "US in Focus: Who Does What in US Immigration." *Migration Information Source*, December 2005. http://www.migrationinformation.org/USFocus/display.cfm?ID=362

Ennis, Sharon R., Merarys Rios-Vargas, and Nora G. Albert. "The Hispanic Population: 2010." United States Census Bureau, May 2011. http://www.hacu.net/images/hacu/OPAI/2012_Virtual_Binder/2010%20census%20brief%20-%20hispanic%20population.pdf

Federation for American Immigration Reform. "Immigration in Arizona: Fact Sheet (2012)." *Immigration Issues*, April 2012. http://www.fairus.org/issue/immigration-in-arizona-fact-sheet

Gibson, Dave. "Illegal Aliens Cost California More Than $1 Billion Annually." Examiner.com, July 11, 2011. http://www.examiner.com/article/illegal-aliens-cost-california-hospitals-more-than-1-billion-annually

Grieco, Elizabeth M., Yesenia D. Acosta, G. Patricia de la Cruz, et al. "The Foreign-Born Population in the United States: 2010." *American Community Survey Reports*, May 2012. http://www.census.gov/prod/2012pubs/acs-19.pdf

Hawley, Chris. "Immigration Has Grown More Complicated." *USA Today*, October 8, 2010. http://usatoday30.usatoday.com/news/world/2010-09-28-migrants28_ST_N.htm

Immigration Policy Center, American Immigration Council. "How the United States Immigration System Works: A Fact Sheet." November 4, 2010. http://www.immigrationpolicy.org/just-facts/how-united-states-immigration-system-works-fact-sheet

Obama, Barack. "Presidential Memorandum—Annual Refugee Admissions Numbers." The White House, September 28, 2012. http://www.whitehouse.gov/the-press-office/2012/09/28/presidential-memorandum-annual-refugee-admissions-numbers

Sbarra, Silvano. Personal interview with author, December 2012.

Smith, Fraser. Personal interview with author, December 2012.

Smith, Lamar. "Immigration Enforcement and Border Security Are the First Line Defense Against Terrorists." Foxnews.com, September 12, 2011. http://www.foxnews.com/opinion/2011/09/12/next-10-years-immigration-enforcement-and-border-security-are-first-line/

United States District Court, Southern District of New York. "Naturalization Ceremony and Schedule." http://www.nysd.uscourts.gov/naturalization.php

US Citizenship and Immigration Services. "Citizenship through Naturalization." January 22, 2013. http://www.uscis.gov/portal/site/uscis/menuitem.eb1d4c2a3e5b9ac89243c6a7543f6d1a/?vgnextoid=d84d6811264a3210VgnVCM100000b92ca60aRCRD&vgnextchannel=d84d6811264a3210VgnVCM100000b92ca60aRCRD

US Citizenship and Immigration Services. "Civics (History and Government) Questions for the Naturalization Test." March 2011. http://www.uscis.gov/USCIS/Office%20of%20Citizenship/Citizenship%20Resource%20Center%20Site/Publications/100q.pdf

US Citizenship and Immigration Services. "Green Card (Permanent Residence)." May 13, 2011. http://www.uscis.gov/greencard

US Citizenship and Immigration Services. http://www.uscis.gov/

US Citizenship and Immigration Services. "Naturalization Oath of Allegiance to the United States of America." September 4, 2012. http://www.uscis.gov/portal/site/uscis/menuitem.5af9bb95919f35e66f614176543f6d1a/?vgnextoid=facd6db8d7e37210VgnVCM100000082ca60aRCRD&vgnextchannel=dd7ffe9dd4aa3210VgnVCM100000b92ca60aRCRD

US Citizenship and Immigration Services. "Other Ways to Get a Green Card." April 16, 2013. http://www.uscis.gov/portal/site/uscis/menuitem.eb1d4c2a3e5b9ac89243c6a7543f6d1a/?vgnextoid=5a97a6c515083210VgnVCM100000082ca60aRCRD&vgnextchannel=5a97a6c515083210VgnVCM100000082ca60aRCRD

US Citizenship and Immigration Services. "Welcome to the United States: A Guide for New Immigrants." September 2007. http://www.uscis.gov/files/nativedocuments/M-618.pdf

US Citizenship and Immigration Services. "Welcome to USA.gov: Celebrate Citizenship, Learn About America." http://www.welcometousa.gov

US Department of Homeland Security, Office of Immigration Statistics. "2011 Yearbook of Immigration Statistics." September 2012. http://www.dhs.gov/sites/default/files/publications/immigration-statistics/yearbook/2011/ois_yb_2011.pdf

US Department of State. http://travel.state.gov

census (SEN-suhs)—A tally taken every ten years by the US federal government that determines the population of the country and information about the population such as gender or age.

deported (dih-POHRT-id)—Forcibly removed from a country.

descendant (dih-SEN-duhnt)—A person who can trace their ancestry to another person (such as a child, grandchild, or great-grandchild).

green card—The document that allows a person to legally live and work in the United States on a permanent basis.

indentured servant (in-DEN-cherd SUR-vuhnt)—A person who historically did not have the means to pay for passage across the Atlantic, so he or she worked as an unpaid servant for a number of years to pay off that debt.

international (in-ter-NASH-uh-nuhl)—Something that involves more than one country.

immediate family (ih-MEE-dee-it FAM-uh-lee)—Family members including parents, spouses, children, and siblings.

naturalization (nach-er-uh-lahy-ZAY-shuhn)—The process by which a foreign-born person becomes a citizen.

sponsor (SPON-ser)—To support someone or something financially, or to vouch for another person.

visa (VEE-zuh)—A document that gives non-citizens clearance to enter a country and remain there for specified period of time.

About the AUTHOR

Amie Jane Leavitt is an accomplished author and photographer. She graduated from Brigham Young University as an education major and has since taught all subjects and grade levels in both private and public schools. She is an adventurer who loves to travel the globe in search of interesting story ideas and beautiful places to capture in photographs. She has written dozens of books for kids, has contributed to online and print media, and has worked as a consultant, writer, and editor for numerous educational publishing and assessment companies. Amie has a lot of close friends who are either first or second generation Americans. Because of that, she has had a great interest in and appreciation for the immigration process most of her life. It's for that reason, and because of her own heritage as a descendant of immigrants, that she particularly enjoyed researching and writing this book. To see a listing of Amie's current projects and other published works, check out her website at www.amiejaneleavitt.com.

[7]